CORE CHEMISTRY

Fuel and the Environment

DENISE WALKER

A⁺
Smart Apple Media
an imprint of Black Rabbit Books

This book has been published in cooperation with Evans Publishing Group.

Series editor: Harriet Brown, Editor: Katie Harker, Design: Robert Walster, Illustrations: Peter Bull Art Studio, Ian Thompson

Published in the United States by Smart Apple Media
2140 Howard Drive West
North Mankato, Minnesota 56003

Library of Congress Cataloging-in-Publication Data

Walker, Denise.
Fuel and the environment / by Denise Walker.
p. cm. – (Core chemistry)
Includes index.
ISBN 978-1-58340-818-6
1. Fuel. 2. Fossil fuel. 3. Fuel—Environmental aspects. I. Title.

TP318.W35 2007
333.79—dc22   2006103524

9 8 7 6 5 4 3 2 1

Contents

Introduction

Fuel has become an important part of our daily lives. Without fuel, we would be unable to heat our homes or cook food. We depend on fuel to run our cars, buses, trains, and airplanes. Fuel is used to produce electricity and to power lights and appliances in our homes. Refined fuel is also used to make many everyday products.

This book takes you on a journey to discover more about the wonderful world of fuel. Find out about different types of fuel, discover how we access and refine fuel, and learn about the impact that fuel has on the environment. You can also find out about famous scientists, such as Charles Goodyear and Leo Baekeland. Learn how they discovered methods for making rubber and plastic from fuel—materials that have revolutionized our lives.

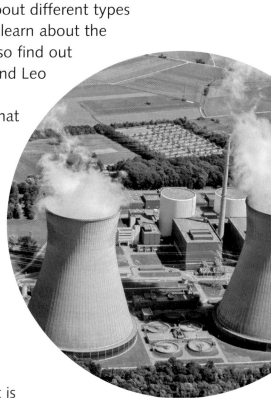

This book contains feature boxes that will help you understand more about fuel and the environment. Test yourself on what you are learning; investigate some of the concepts discussed; find out key facts; and discover some of the scientific findings of the past and how these might be utilized in the future.

Fuel is a vital part of modern life but it is important that we use it responsibly to protect our natural world. Now you can understand why the race is on to find alternative fuels for the future—to replace the fuel that we have used and to minimize its impact on the environment.

DID YOU KNOW?

▶ Look for these boxes. They contain interesting facts about fuel and our environment.

TEST YOURSELF

▶ Use these boxes to see how much you've learned. Try to answer the questions without looking at the book, but take a look if you are really stuck.

INVESTIGATE

▶ These boxes contain experiments that you can carry out at home. The equipment you will need is usually inexpensive and easy to find around the house.

TIME TRAVEL

▶ These boxes describe scientific discoveries from the past and fascinating developments that pave the way for the advance of science in the future.

ANSWERS

On pages 46 and 47, you will find the answers to the questions from the "Test yourself" and "Investigate" boxes.

GLOSSARY

Words highlighted in **bold** are described in detail in the glossary on pages 46 and 47.

What is fuel?

A fuel is a substance that is used to release heat energy, light energy, or both. We use fuel to heat our homes, to cook our food, and to generate electricity. Fuel also runs the vehicles that we use to move people and goods from place to place, around the world, and into space.

▶ We use fuel to make electricity and to power our vehicles.

Fuel releases heat and light energy through **combustion reactions**. It burns in oxygen to release energy, as well as a number of chemical products.

▲ Wood is a traditional fuel used for cooking and heating.

Many of the fuels that we use in everyday life are **fossil fuels**. Fossil fuels are made from the remains of prehistoric plants and animals that have been buried beneath the earth's surface over millions of years. Fossil fuels, such as **crude oil**, coal, and natural gas, have been used for thousands of years. As long ago as 1500 B.C., the Chinese and Egyptians burned oil to light their lamps.

DIFFERENT TYPES OF FUEL

Throughout history, different substances have been used as fuel. The type of fuel that is utilized depends upon the available resources in a particular area. Here are examples of the types of fuel that we use.

▶ Coal—In 2005, coal provided about 26 percent of the energy needed worldwide. Most coal supplies are used to generate electricity. China and the United States are rich in coal deposits, but scientists estimate that, at current rates of consumption, the worldwide coal supply will only last another 252 years.

▶ Crude oil—In 2005, oil provided about 35 percent of the world's energy needs. Almost 90 percent of vehicles are powered by gasoline or diesel fuel, which are **refined** products of crude oil. Oil is also used to generate electricity, and it is an important ingredient in many industrial chemicals. However, there are only an estimated 32 years of oil supplies left.

▶ Natural gas—In 2005, natural gas provided about 25 percent of the world's energy needs.

Gas is used for heating homes and for some industrial processes. Natural gas is transported through pipelines and costs about the same as gasoline. Natural gas has been a plentiful fuel, but scientists think the supply will be exhausted in about 72 years.

▶ Propane—Propane is found in crude oil and in natural gas. It is commonly used in a gaseous state for heating, cooking, lighting, and industrial purposes. In a liquid state, propane is also used to fuel vehicles.

▶ Ethanol—Ethanol is made by **fermenting** sugar from corn or sugar cane. In the U.S. and Brazil, ethanol has been used for many years as a fuel to power vehicles by combining it with gasoline (see page 37).

▶ Methanol—Methanol is a **compound** similar to ethanol and is made from the fermentation of sugars or from wood. Methanol burns efficiently, so it is sometimes mixed with gasoline and used as a fuel for high-performance racing cars.

▶ Biomass—**Biomass** describes energy from the sun that is incorporated into animals and plants by the **food chain**. Sources of biomass include farming waste and animal feces. Biomass can also generate electricity (see page 45).

FOSSIL FUELS

Three of the most important fuels that we use today are coal, crude oil, and natural gas. Crude oil and natural gas form over millions of years from the remains of dead animals; coal comes from dead plant remains. Fossil fuels are **nonrenewable** fuels because they are consumed faster than they can be replaced. This means that fossil fuels are in danger of running out.

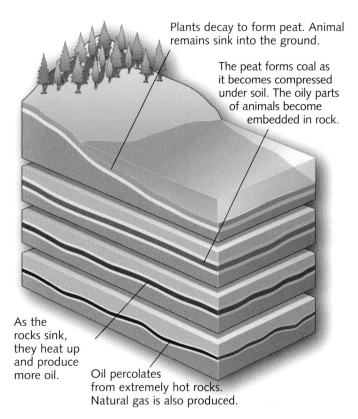

Plants decay to form peat. Animal remains sink into the ground.

The peat forms coal as it becomes compressed under soil. The oily parts of animals become embedded in rock.

As the rocks sink, they heat up and produce more oil.

Oil percolates from extremely hot rocks. Natural gas is also produced.

▲ Fossil fuels form over millions of years from the remains of dead plants and animals.

DID YOU KNOW?

▶ Scientists have calculated how much energy we use to fuel our cars in comparison to the remains of dead animals. The average car tank can hold 14.5 gallons (55 l) of fuel—this is equivalent to the distilled remains of 225 elephants! These figures may seem high, but fuel is only made from a small percentage of an animal's remains (on average, 1 part in 10,000). These remains begin to form a fuel over the course of about 500 million years.

▶ In prehistoric times, people saw mysterious fires coming from the ground. These fires were thought to be signs from the gods or symbolic of an invisible god. Today, scientists believe that the fires were probably fueled by natural gas. For example, during a thunderstorm, it would be possible for lightning to ignite natural gas that had escaped from beneath the earth's crust.

HYDROCARBONS

Fossil fuels are also called **hydrocarbons**. In their pure form, hydrocarbons contain only carbon and hydrogen—elements that are released from the remains of dead organisms.

When hydrocarbons burn, they release energy in the form of heat and light, and they release chemical products. The hydrogen in the hydrocarbon burns in oxygen to form water, which is released as steam because the reaction occurs at a high temperature. The carbon in the fuel burns in oxygen and releases carbon dioxide. If the fuel is burning in a small amount of oxygen, carbon monoxide may be released instead.

DEMONSTRATING COMPLETE COMBUSTION

If fuel burns in a sufficient supply of oxygen, we say that complete combustion occurs—all of the hydrocarbons in the fuel burn to produce their chemical products. The diagram below shows that the products of complete combustion are carbon dioxide and water.

When the candle is lit, it is placed very close to the funnel, so it will burn with a strong orange flame and produce little smoke. This shows that almost complete combustion is occurring. The candle wax is an example of hydrocarbon fuel. It is useful for this experiment because we can control the amount of fuel that is used.

When the water pump is turned on, air from the burning candle is drawn through the equipment. The air contains the products of combustion. First, the air passes through a chilled, empty U-tube. This causes the components to **condense**. The air then passes through limewater and we see a lot of bubbles. The limewater quickly turns milky, indicating the presence of carbon dioxide.

At the end of the experiment, the U-tube contains a colorless liquid. If this liquid is added to anhydrous cobalt chloride, the solution turns pink, indicating the presence of water.

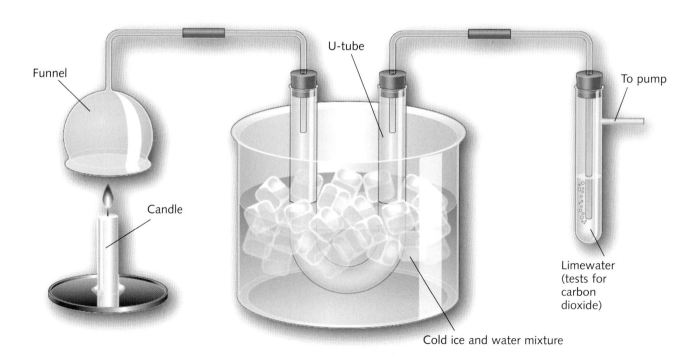

Funnel

Candle

U-tube

To pump

Limewater (tests for carbon dioxide)

Cold ice and water mixture

DEMONSTRATING INCOMPLETE COMBUSTION

If the candle is too close to the funnel, it produces much more smoke because the funnel limits the supply of oxygen. This smoke is unburned carbon. The limewater remains unchanged and colorless for much longer, indicating that very little carbon dioxide has been released. Instead, a deadly gas called carbon monoxide (CO) is produced; however, water is still collected.

Complete and incomplete combustion can be observed in a laboratory with a Bunsen burner. If the air hole of a burner is opened, there is a good supply of oxygen and complete combustion occurs. The flame is bright blue and no soot is evident, which means carbon is not present. If the air hole is only partially opened, the supply of oxygen is lower. In this instance, the products are water and carbon (soot), some carbon monoxide, and much less carbon dioxide.

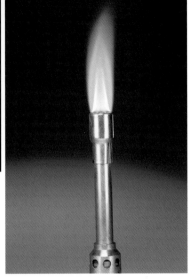

▲ ▶ An orange flame on a Bunsen burner indicates incomplete combustion, while a bright blue flame indicates complete combustion, due to a plentiful supply of oxygen.

CARBON MONOXIDE

Incomplete combustion occurs in many of the gasoline-fueled vehicles on our roads. This is evident when clouds of black smoke are expelled from exhaust pipes. Some vehicles carry out both incomplete and complete combustion—both carbon dioxide and carbon monoxide are released from the exhaust.

Carbon monoxide is a deadly gas that is difficult to detect because it is colorless and odorless. Carbon monoxide interferes with the transportation of oxygen around the body. When we breathe in carbon monoxide, the gas binds to the red blood cells in our body—blood cells that usually carry oxygen gas. If enough red blood cells are bonded with carbon monoxide molecules, it can be fatal.

Fortunately, when gasoline fumes reach the atmosphere, the carbon monoxide is dispersed in the air and becomes less dangerous. However, carbon monoxide can be a problem in our homes if gas appliances are faulty and there is poor ventilation. Gas stoves and furnaces should be inspected regularly to ensure complete combustion is taking place.

2

Extracting fossil fuels

Fossil fuels are generally found deep beneath the earth's surface; therefore, their extraction is not always easy. Over time, various techniques have been developed to obtain these important fuels.

COAL

Coal forms from the remains of prehistoric trees, ferns, and other plants. Over millions of years, the remains are crushed into the earth and compressed by layers of rocks and sediment. Slowly, the remains decay and coal is left behind.

Coal is formed in stages. The initial form of coal is called peat. This soft, brown material is similar to coal but has had less time to compress and decompose. Peat contains about 70 percent water. It is found near the earth's surface and is sometimes used as fuel for heating homes and for cooking.

▲ Peat is found near the earth's surface and can be harvested using farm machinery.

If peat is left in the ground it becomes lignite—the next stage of coal formation. Lignite is much harder than peat. It contains approximately 55 percent carbon and 35 percent water. Eventually, anthracite is formed. This very hard material is almost 100 percent carbon; anthracite is the highest grade of coal.

The U.S. has the world's largest known coal reserves—about 303 billion tons (275 billion t). However, since scientists believe that world coal reserves will decline dramatically over the next 250 years, this resource will be more heavily drawn upon. Each year, the U.S. mines around 1.1 billion tons (1 billion t) of coal—the United Kingdom (UK) mines 110 million tons (100 million t).

COAL EXTRACTION

In the U.S. and the UK, most coal deposits are found at a depth of several hundred feet. The coal is extracted from underground mines. Mines are holes drilled under the earth's surface that are large enough to hold people and vehicles. The mines are supported with steel frames to protect the miners from collapsing earth. Coal is removed from the rock surrounding the mine and transported to the surface.

▼ This technician is measuring the noise levels produced by machinery in a coal mine. Mine workers have to wear ear protectors to prevent hearing loss.

▲ Heavy machinery is used to excavate coal at this surface coal mine in central Asia.

In other parts of the world, where coal is much closer to the surface, surface mining is the preferred method of extraction. This method uses heavy machinery to move surface earth in order to excavate the coal. This type of mining creates piles of earth called spoil banks.

In areas where coal is buried very deep, a new type of coal mining, called mountaintop removal, has been developed. In some regions of the world, mountaintop removal is the only way more coal can be extracted. The tops of hills are excavated to 985 feet (300 m), and the remaining land is leveled using explosives. This type of mining is very destructive to the environment.

USES FOR COAL

Today, around 80 percent of coal is used in power stations to generate electricity. Coal also powers industrial processes, such as steelmaking furnaces. Some people use coal furnaces to heat their homes. Many countries also export their coal reserves for these uses.

Coal is often refined to make it a cleaner fuel. When coal is heated in the absence of air, impurities, such as coal tar and coal gas, are removed. Refined coal is called "coke," which burns without producing smoke.

TIME TRAVEL: DISCOVERIES OF THE PAST

▶ Scientists have developed a technique that produces synthetic oil from coal or natural gas. In the Fischer-Tropsch process, a mixture of carbon monoxide and hydrogen—from coal or gas—reacts to produce a synthetic fuel oil. The technique is often used in countries, such as South Africa, that are rich in coal deposits.

The process was first invented in Germany during the 1920s. Although Germany had very little fuel, it had large coal deposits. Today, a handful of companies are using the technology. Sasol, for example, produces most of South Africa's diesel fuel by combining coal and natural gas resources. This technology is likely to become increasingly important as oil deposits decline.

In the 1800s, before oil was used commercially, animal fats, such as whale fat, were burned in torches and lamps to produce heat and light. However, animal fats were expensive—an equivalent of $198 per gallon (3.8 l) at today's prices—so only the wealthy could afford them. People began to search for cheaper fuel alternatives, and in 1857, Michael Dietz invented the kerosene lamp. Kerosene was initially refined from oil that had seeped from the ground or that could be extracted from rocks. It was cheaper than whale fat, burned cleanly, smelled better, and it did not decompose. Kerosene lamps were used until the electric light bulb was invented in 1879.

FINDING OIL

China was probably the first country to use oil. In around A.D. 300, China is known to have extracted oil by drilling a hole to a depth of more than 655 feet (200 m), using a drill attached to a bamboo pole. The Chinese used the heat from burning oil to evaporate water from brine to produce salt. The more modern approach to oil extraction began in the 1800s.

In 1855, the first oil wells were opened in Ontario, Canada. By 1910, a number of large Canadian oil reserves were being explored. During this time, oil wells were also opened in the East Indies, Persia (present-day Iran), Peru, and Venezuela. The demand for oil increased around the world—largely due to the invention of motor vehicles.

Oil has been extracted from the ground for more than 100 years and supplies are becoming increasingly difficult to find. Locating a source of oil is a precise science. Although oil naturally rises to the surface in some parts of the world—such as in remote parts of Alaska—more precise exploratory techniques need to be devised.

When an exploration company looks for a new oil source, it searches for obvious surface features, such as oil or gas seeps—natural springs where oil or natural gas leaks out of the ground. There are also features called "pockmarks" that form when natural gas escapes in these regions.

▲ This heavy oil is seeping through the sand at Vernal, Utah. An estimated 28 billion barrels of oil are thought to be available from sand deposits in Utah.

If the surface features are not apparent, a company will rely on more sophisticated methods. Aerial and satellite photographs may indicate geographical features that suggest the presence of oil or gas. If this is the case, the first test will be a gravity and magnetic survey. In a gravity survey, a gravimeter is used to detect changes in the earth's gravitational field. These changes are due to small vibrations caused by the activity of fuel within the earth. During a magnetic search, a magnetometer is used to measure the strength of the earth's magnetic field. These changes are caused by the presence of rocks beneath the earth's surface and might signify the presence of oil.

▲ A computer representation of oil deposits (shown in red) in rocks beneath the earth's surface.

If the results of these searches indicate possible fuel deposits, a seismic survey will be conducted. During a seismic survey, sound waves are projected into the earth's crust and scientists record the time it takes for them to be reflected back from the rocks underground. This determines the types of rocks that are beneath the earth's surface and their densities.

The last stage in finding oil is an experimental drill. If the seismic survey is encouraging, an experimental hole is drilled. If oil is found, mass **spectroscopy** can also be used to test the molecules in an oil sample. This determines the age of the sample and helps the oil company decide the logistics of bringing oil to the surface. The whole process is very expensive and there is no guarantee that oil will be extracted. Once oil has been found, the cost of setting up a well to extract the oil ranges from $1 million to more than $100 million.

OIL EXTRACTION

Once an oil deposit has been discovered, it will be extracted in four stages:

(1) Drilling—An oil rig drills a hole between 4 to 30 inches (10–75 cm) wide. A metal pipe, slightly smaller than the hole, is inserted to ensure the hole will not collapse. The hole is then drilled deeper. This process is repeated until a suitable depth is reached. Sometimes, oil rigs are constructed at sea. These "offshore" oil rigs can be the size of small towns, and workers live on the rigs for months at a time.
(2) Completion—Holes are drilled in the side of the metal piping to allow oil from surrounding rocks to flow into the main hole. Acids and fluids are injected into the main drill hole to encourage the oil flow from the surrounding rocks.
(3) Production—Oil and gas are extracted. The high pressure in the narrow drill hole causes oil to rise to the surface. Oil is also extracted from the ground using a mechanical pump.
(4) Abandonment—Once all the oil has been extracted, the well is abandoned and the hole is filled with cement.

▲ A drilling rig can be used to drill hundreds of feet into the ground.

▼ "Nodding donkeys" are a type of pump used to extract oil from beneath the earth's surface.

TRANSPORTING FOSSIL FUELS

Once crude oil, natural gas, and coal are mined, they need to be transported to consumers. Unfortunately, transporting fuel can cause environmental damage. Mining itself can be destructive to the environment, and transportation can make the problem worse. Some of the environmental concerns associated with mining are outlined below.

▶ Dust pollution—One of the consequences of a mine explosion is the fallout dust that follows. Local residents who are sensitive to dust may become more vulnerable to lung diseases, such as asthma.

▶ Air pollution—Trucks and other vehicles that transport fossil fuels increase the amount of dust and exhaust fumes that pollute the air.

▶ Destruction of land and habitat—When a mine is abandoned, the surrounding land may never return to its original state. This is especially true when mountaintop removal is used to extract coal. If the landscape has been altered, local habitats will suffer, sometimes permanently. Mining also leaves behind waste materials, such as scrap metal, acids, solvents, and diesel fuel.

▶ Noise pollution—Explosives used to free fossil fuels from rock are very loud. This disturbs people and animals living nearby.

▲ Mining blasts produce both air and noise pollution, causing difficulties for those living nearby.

TIME TRAVEL: INTO THE FUTURE

▶ Scientists have been researching ways to drill for oil and gas that are kinder to the environment. In the future, powerful laser beams of light may be used to drill into the ground. Scientists are also looking at ways to send robots to the bottom of the ocean to drill for oil, instead of building large offshore oil rigs.

▶ The Arctic could be a useful new source of natural gas. Scientists have found samples of natural gas in wet snow and ice in the Arctic region, and it is believed that more gas lies undiscovered in the area. However, there are concerns that extracting the gas could cause serious damage to this natural habitat.

▲ Oil tankers are an inexpensive way to transport oil, but an oil spill could be environmentally and economically costly.

TRANSPORTATION

Pipelines were first used to move oil and natural gas around the world in the late 1800s. Once a pipeline is established, it is an economical way to transport oil and gas. Pipelines are less expensive than using highways or railroads because large quantities of fuel can be continuously transported.

Pipelines are mostly used on land. They can be built under the sea, but construction is difficult and tanker ships may be more economical. Oil is transported using either steel or plastic pipes that vary from one to four feet (0.3–1.2 m) in diameter.

▼ Pumps are used to move oil through pipelines at average speeds of 13 feet (4 m) per second.

Pipelines are usually built above the ground, but when they are close to urban or environmentally-sensitive areas, they are buried about three feet (1 m) underground. Natural gas pipelines follow the same guidelines as oil pipelines, but the diameter of gas pipes is slightly smaller.

Pipelines transport valuable fuel around the world, but they have one major disadvantage—fuel is explosive. When explosive material is transported, there is always the risk of an accident. For example, in 1989, sparks from two passing trains ignited a gas leak from a pipeline in Russia, killing 645 people. Pipelines must be regularly inspected to prevent accidents of this kind. Pipelines may also be vulnerable to terrorist attacks.

DID YOU KNOW?

▶ A 746-mile (1,200 km) pipeline runs along the seabed from Norway to the UK. Natural gas travels along this pipeline at about 15 miles (24 km) per hour.
▶ Ships that carry oil and gas are constructed so that they are less likely to leak if a collision occurs. The tankers have a "double hull" as added protection. Empty spaces in the hull are also filled with a type of gas that is not flammable.

3

Refining fossil fuels

Chemists have discovered a variety of uses for crude oil, natural gas, and coal. Once these fossil fuels are transported from their source, they are converted to products for consumers.

USES FOR FOSSIL FUELS

▶ Transportation—Internal combustion engines are used in a variety of modern vehicles, from cars to trains. These engines use the energy from ignited gasoline or diesel fuel to move pistons. In airplanes, aviation fuel powers jet engines. These fuels are all types of refined crude oil.

▲ Airplane engines use a type of refined crude oil.

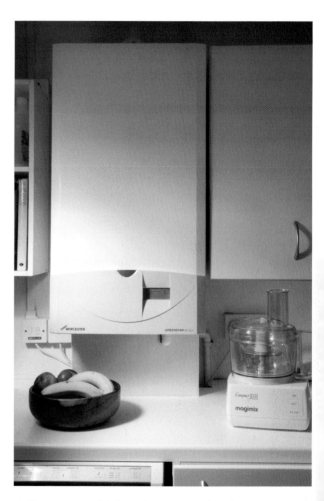

▲ Furnaces provide heat for most modern homes.

▶ Heating—Some people burn coal to heat their homes. However, many homes now use central heating, powered by natural gas or electricity. Houses are built with a system of ducts that are connected to a furnace. When the furnace is on, the gas or electricity releases heat energy. This heat energy warms the air that is pushed through the heating ducts to other rooms in the house.

▶ Electricity—Most power stations use combustible fuels, such as coal and oil, to heat water and turn it into steam. The steam drives the turbines (giant rotating shafts) in a generator, which converts the movement into an electrical current. A network of power lines then transports the electricity to places where it is needed.

▶ Manufactured materials—Plastic is one of the most common and versatile materials in the world. Produced from crude oil, plastic is a relatively new material (see page 24). Oil is also used to manufacture paint, fertilizer, medicine, lubricants, rubber tires, and candles.

▶ Cooking—Most stoves are powered by electricity or natural gas. The natural gas in stoves is mainly composed of **methane**, and it is similar to the gas used for Bunsen burners. Natural gas is odorless, and for safety reasons, a natural chemical odorant is added, which smells like rotten eggs. The strong smell helps detect dangerous gas leaks.

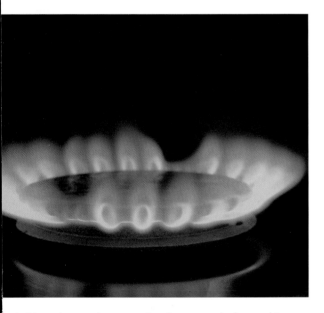

▲ Many homes have a natural gas supply for cooking and heating.

Other fuels used for cooking include butane and propane. These gaseous fuels are cooled, converting them to a liquid state. Butane and propane are stored in canisters for camping stoves and outdoor grills. Both of these fuels are also derived from crude oil.

SMOKELESS FUELS

During the 1800s, a lot of coal was burned for heat and power, but the air became heavily polluted with black dust and smoke. Today, some towns and cities in the UK only allow "smokeless" fuel to be used in homes. Coke is an example of a smokeless fuel. Coke is difficult to light, but it burns with a "clean," blue flame, and produces only a small amount of soot. To make smokeless fuels, coal is heated in an enclosed environment to drive off pollutant tars. While it is still hot, the coke is shaped into convenient briquettes.

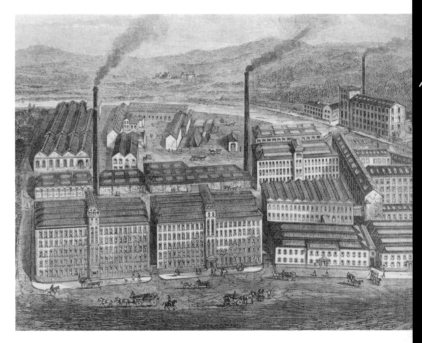

▲ During the Industrial Revolution of the eighteenth and nineteenth centuries, factories produced smoke pollution as their productivity increased.

INVESTIGATE

▶ The fuels we choose often depend on the amount of energy they produce. Ask your teacher to help you to compare the amount of energy in ethanol and paraffin wax.

Burn equal quantities of each fuel to heat two beakers of water. Test the temperature of the water in each beaker before and after the experiment. Which fuel heats the water the most?

REFINING CRUDE OIL

Crude oil is composed of hydrocarbons from prehistoric organisms buried in the earth. The hydrocarbon compounds contain only hydrogen and carbon atoms. Some hydrocarbons are described as "short-chain" because they contain very few carbon and hydrogen atoms. Other hydrocarbons are described as "long-chain" because they are composed of many atoms, forming long chains.

In its unrefined form, crude oil is not very useful. However, crude oil's hydrocarbon compounds can be very valuable. Drilling companies will either sell the crude oil to another company for refining or refine it themselves. The latter is more profitable because oil companies can sell the products of the refined crude oil.

FRACTIONAL DISTILLATION OF CRUDE OIL

When crude oil is refined, it is heated and passed through fractional distillation equipment that separates the oil's components according to their boiling points. The oil undergoes each of the following stages:

(1) Crude oil is heated as it passes into the column. The hydrocarbons that are shortest will evaporate first because they have the lowest boiling points. The vapor will travel to the top of the column before condensing and being collected. Typically this fraction produces no more than four carbon atoms and is called petroleum gas.

(2) The hydrocarbons with the next lowest boiling point will evaporate and travel to the top of the column. This fraction has between 4 and 8 carbon atoms and is called gasoline—the fuel used to power cars.

FRACTIONAL DISTILLATION

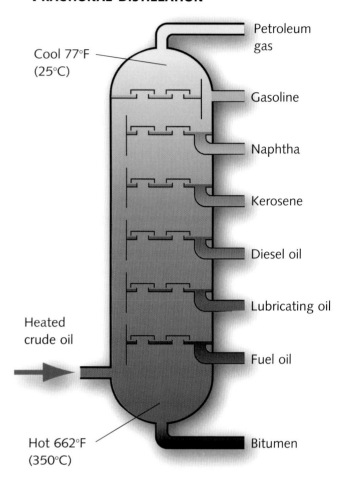

▲ When crude oil is refined using fractional distillation, eight different fractions of oil can be collected.

(3) The remaining fractions evaporate as their boiling points are reached, and then separated.

The fractions that follow gasoline are
(1) Naphtha (8–10 carbon atoms),
(2) Kerosene (10–16 carbon atoms),
(3) Diesel oil (16–20 carbon atoms),
(4) Lubricating oil (20–30 carbon atoms),
(5) Fuel oil (30–40 carbon atoms),
(6) Bitumen (more than 50 carbon atoms).

Each of these fractions has its own individual uses, summarized in the table on page 19.

Fraction	Use
Petroleum gas	Used to make methane
Gasoline	Fuel for cars
Naphtha	Used to make chemicals and medicines
Kerosene	Fuel for aircraft
Diesel oil	Central heating and vehicle fuel
Lubricating oil	Oil for machinery
Fuel oil	Fuel for power stations
Bitumen	Surfacing for roads

TEST YOURSELF

(1) Mark distills crude oil in a laboratory but is confused about the order of the fractions that he has separated. How can Mark identify the fractions?

(2) Write down all the fractions of crude oil on different pieces of paper. Shuffle the papers and try to put the fractions in order of increasing mass.

LABORATORY DISTILLATION OF OIL

Fractional distillation can be replicated in a laboratory on a much smaller scale. Sometimes scientists soak a sample of glass wool with crude oil and heat it using a Bunsen burner. When the first oil fraction evaporates, it condenses into a small test tube that is then removed and replaced with another tube for the next fraction. Another way to carry out fractional distillation is to use a glass column filled with glass beads. As the oil evaporates it passes through the column and the beads provide a large, cool surface area on which the oil fraction condenses, forming a liquid. The heat then causes the liquid to evaporate again and recondense farther up the column, where it can be collected.

As each fraction is collected, they become increasingly dark in color with a thicker consistency. These properties result from the number of carbon atoms in each fraction—the larger the number of carbon atoms, the darker and thicker the fraction.

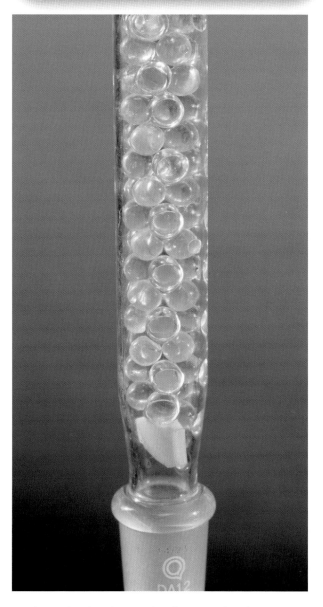

▲ These glass beads provide a large, cool surface area on which the fractions of evaporated oil can condense. Oil can be separated in a laboratory on a small scale.

USING THE FRACTIONS

▶ Gasoline—Gasoline is used as fuel for a majority of the world's automobiles. Before the invention of cars in the mid-1800s, gasoline was sold in small vials and primarily used as a treatment for lice.

Additives are put into gasoline to make it even more useful. The table below shows some uses for gasoline additives:

Additive	Reason
Lead	Prevented gasoline from igniting in the engine too soon. No longer used because of the dangers of lead poisoning.
MMT (methyl-cyclopentadienyl manganese tricarbonyl)	Allows cars designed to run on leaded fuel to run on unleaded fuel, which is better for the environment.
Oxygenates	Reduces the amount of carbon monoxide produced in the exhaust fumes.

▶ Kerosene—Kerosene was traditionally used in kerosene lamps before the invention of electricity. Today, kerosene is used as an aviation fuel and in portable camping stoves. Kerosene has more carbon atoms in its molecules than gasoline, so kerosene molecules are bigger. The larger molecules easily combine and are difficult to separate, making kerosene thicker than gasoline. Kerosene's large molecules have higher boiling and melting points because more energy is required to separate the individual molecules.

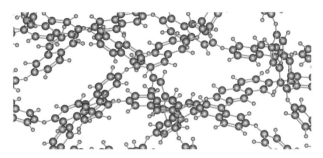

▲ Heavy molecules of oil are tangled and difficult to separate. This makes the liquid very thick.

▶ Diesel oil—Diesel can be pumped and is a useful fuel for running vehicles. Because diesel is thicker than kerosene, it is also a good lubricant for the engine. Larger vehicles usually run on diesel because it burns efficiently over long distances. In the 1930s, one of the first diesel vehicles was driven for nearly 746 miles (1,200 km) without stopping! Diesel vehicles have a reputation for being "sluggish," but technology has improved to such an extent that in the last two decades, some racing cars have begun to use diesel fuel. In 2006, a British diesel-powered vehicle broke records by reaching speeds of around 348 miles (560 km) per hour.

▶ Fuel oil—This product is so thick, it barely classifies as a liquid. Fuel oil is used to power ships that travel great distances. It burns slowly and releases a lot of energy. However, it does not burn cleanly, so it is unsuitable for use in towns and cities.

▶ Lubricating oil—Lubricating oil is thicker than diesel. It is also more slick, or smooth, than diesel oil. Because of this, it is used to lubricate the surfaces of moving parts. Lubricated surfaces move more freely, preventing friction

▲ Car engines require regular oil changes to keep the parts moving smoothly and to prevent excessive wear.

from wearing them out. Lubricating oils can also prevent the formation of rust on machinery.

▶ Bitumen—Bitumen is the fraction of crude oil that has the highest boiling point. The molecules in bitumen are long-chain, and because they become tangled, bitumen is classified as a solid. Bitumen is used for paving roads because it is strong enough to withstand heavy traffic. Also, bitumen is waterproof, so it is used for roof construction; this is especially important on flat roofs, to prevent leaks in wet weather.

▶ Naphtha—Naphtha is mainly used in the manufacture of chemicals and medicines. It is sometimes an ingredient in shoe polish and a fuel for portable stoves and lanterns.

PARAFFIN WAX

Paraffin wax is also made from crude oil. The molecules in paraffin wax have a lot of carbon atoms; paraffin molecules are in a very tangled long-chain arrangement. They are considered to be in a solid state because so much energy is required to untangle the mass of molecules. Paraffin wax is used to make candles, moisturizers, and food additives. Paraffin wax is also added to candy to make it appear shiny.

CRACKING

Some fractions of crude oil are in high demand. For example, lubricating oil is less useful than gasoline. It is possible for oil companies to refine fractions, creating more product to meet public demand. Gasoline can be produced by separating the heavier oils again, thus splitting their long carbon chains. This process is called catalytic cracking.

▲ Many candles are made from paraffin wax. This fuel is useful because it burns very slowly.

▲ The Grangemouth oil refinery in Scotland is situated near a major waterway where it can easily import crude oil and export refined oil product through tankers and pipelines in the North Sea.

OIL REFINERY LOCATIONS

Oil refineries process millions of gallons of oil that have been drilled from the earth's crust. Choosing the location of an oil refinery is not an easy task because a number of environmental and safety concerns need to be considered.

The world's first oil refinery was opened in 1856 in Romania (with investment from the U.S.). Many more refineries were built in Europe, but during World War II, they were heavily bombed. Today, the world's largest oil refinery is in Saudi Arabia. It was built in Abqaiq, a city originally designed as a seaport, which made it an ideal location for a refinery.

Oil refineries are often located on coasts, away from busy cities. When choosing the location for an oil refinery, the following factors are considered.

▶ Air pollution—Although industries are regulated by strict laws regarding the amount of pollution they release into the atmosphere, oil refineries emit a number of polluting gases. To reduce the effects of air pollution on people, refineries should be built away from populated areas. The refinery should be situated so that prevailing winds do not carry pollution in the direction of towns and cities.

▶ Water pollution—Some refineries use water from local rivers and streams for cooling. The water is pumped out of a river or stream, circulated around the refinery's cooling tower, and returned to the river at a higher temperature. This increase in water temperature is called thermal pollution. Some species of fish are unable to survive in these conditions. Waste products from a refinery may also be washed into local rivers and streams.

▶ Noise pollution—Machinery that operates 24 hours a day makes a lot of noise for people living nearby. Trucks and trains that transport the refined products also contribute to noise pollution.

▶ Transportation—Refineries must be near railroads, highways, or seaports and close to the site where the oil has been drilled.

▶ Special sites of interest—Like other buildings, oil refineries must avoid areas of special scientific interest. These include regions where animals are being protected.

▶ Available workforce—While oil refineries are ideally built in unpopulated areas, a refinery does need workers who live in the vicinity.

▶ Available customers—Oil refineries should be able to deliver products efficiently. Good transportation routes are essential. Some refineries use pipelines to transport their products.

THE EFFECTS OF HURRICANE KATRINA

Sometimes, the production and refining of oil is interrupted by damage from natural disasters. In 2005, the destructive force of Hurricane Katrina in the Mississippi Delta caused some offshore oil rigs to sink and others to be set adrift and disappear. Pipelines ruptured, storage facilities were battered, and many oil refineries had to be shut down. Events like these cost the U.S. government many billions of dollars and disrupt the world's economy. When choosing the location of a new oil refinery, the potential for natural disasters should be taken into consideration.

TEST YOURSELF

▶ Study the diagram of this fictitious island. Imagine you work for an oil company and it is your job to find a location for a new refinery that will process oil from the sea. Where on the island would you build the refinery? Give reasons for your choice.

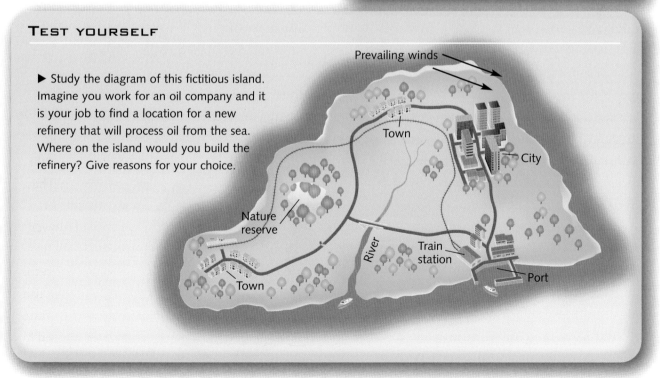

4

Making plastics

Fossil fuels are known for their ability to power our world. However, in recent years, fossil fuels have been used to produce a number of common, everyday materials. Plastic is an everyday material made from fossil fuels. Cooking utensils, furniture, garbage cans, and traffic cones are all made from varieties of plastic. Plastics are manufactured from crude oil through a process called **polymerization**.

DISCOVERING PLASTICS

Many plastics found in nature, such as cellulose and rubber, have been used for centuries, but these products form a small fraction of the plastics that are available today. Scientists have studied the properties of these natural plastics and have tried to improve upon them. In 1839, legend says that an American inventor named Charles Goodyear was experimenting with sulfur and rubber, and he accidentally dropped a piece of sulfur into the rubber mixture. His mistake caused the rubber to become much stronger and able to withstand high temperatures. This substance became known as vulcanized rubber and it was the perfect material for automobile tires.

▲ Charles Goodyear

▲ Telephones used to be made from bakelite plastic.

discovered that they formed a sticky mass when heated but then cooled to a hard substance. Baekeland had invented the first plastic that held its shape after being heated. Bakelite is an effective insulation material. It was used to cover electrical wires and make billiard balls.

Today, some plastics are made by chemically altering the composition of oil. Oils that have hydrogen atoms removed from their carbon chains have weaker links between their atoms and can easily be converted into other products, such as plastics.

◀ Leo Baekeland

MAKING PLASTICS

The boom in plastics manufacturing did not begin until the early 1900s, with the discovery of a new plastic called Bakelite. In 1907, a Belgian-American chemist named Leo Baekeland mixed two chemicals: phenol and formaldehyde. He

When plastics are produced, the molecules in hydrocarbons are linked to form a chain called a polymer. Some hydrocarbons, called alkenes, have double bonds between their atoms. Ethylene is an example of an alkene and has the formula C_2H_4. The two carbon atoms are connected with a double bond.

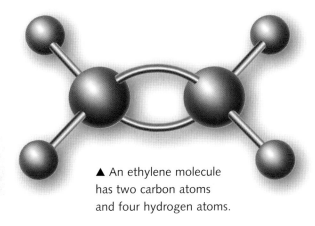

▲ An ethylene molecule has two carbon atoms and four hydrogen atoms.

When ethylene molecules are compressed and a catalyst is added, one of the bonds breaks and links to another ethylene molecule. In this way, hundreds or thousands of molecules are bonded in a long chain, called polyethylene. Polymers, such as polyethylene, are very strong and can be made into a variety of products, such as toys and plastic bottles.

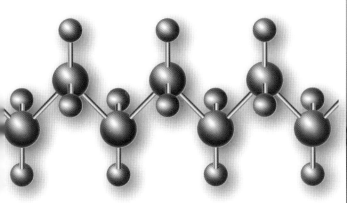

▲ During polymerization, ethylene molecules link to form a strong plastic called polyethylene.

▲ Polymers are used to make everyday plastic materials.

PLASTICS AND THE ENVIRONMENT

One of the advantages of plastic is that it is very durable. Plastics break down slowly and they are generally resistant to physical or chemical attack. However, this material has negative effects on the environment, making its disposal difficult. Plastics are disposed of in two ways:

▶ Plastics are buried in landfills. Because they are **nonbiodegradable**, plastics remain in the ground for hundreds of years. This creates a damaged landscape, renders the land useless for other purposes, and interrupts the natural carbon cycle.

▶ Plastic can be burned. This method instantly disposes of unwanted plastic, but burning plastic releases **toxic** gases into the atmosphere.

▲ Plastics remain in a landfill site for hundreds of years.

The production of plastic is not without environmental problems. Many plastics are made from fossil fuels, and fossil fuels also heat some of the chemical reactions that produce plastics. These fuels release polluting chemicals into the atmosphere.

SOLUTIONS TO THE ENVIRONMENTAL PROBLEMS

In the 1990s, plastic **recycling** programs became widespread, especially in the U.S. Plastics are separated from regular trash, melted down, and remolded into new plastics. Unfortunately, not all plastics are suitable for recycling—plastic that can be recycled is marked with a "recycling" symbol.

The greatest drawback of plastic recycling is that the process is labor-intensive. The varieties of plastic must be sorted before they are treated. This is usually accomplished by hand. Another drawback is that recycling plastic is not always cost-effective; for example, polystyrene is rarely recycled.

To address these problems, scientists have designed some biodegradable plastics. These plastics will decompose more readily when exposed to sunlight. However, the main disadvantage is that the carbon molecules in the plastic are released into the atmosphere as carbon dioxide gas, which contributes to **global warming** (see page 29). For now, biodegradable plastics are too expensive for everyday use.

> ### TEST YOURSELF
>
> ▶ One of the advantages of plastic has been its low cost compared to other materials, such as glass and metal. However, the cost of plastic has risen dramatically in recent years. Why do you think this is?

The cost of fuel

Fossil fuels are nonrenewable fuels. This means that they are being consumed more quickly than they can be produced. Every day, we use about 320 billion kilowatt-hours of energy—the equivalent of approximately 22 lightbulbs constantly glowing for every person on the planet. Such high energy demands cannot be satisfied by existing fossil fuel supplies.

WHERE ARE FOSSIL FUELS FOUND?

The largest oil reserves in the world are in Venezuela, South America, which also has the second largest natural gas reserves in the western hemisphere. Venezuela exports some of this oil to the U.S. and supplies about 15 percent of U.S. energy requirements. Venezuela's oil exports comprise around half of the government's annual revenue. In 2006, a barrel of Venezuelan crude oil was worth more than $50.

Venezuelan natural gas, although plentiful, is not distributed as successfully as its crude oil because of inadequate transportation. Approximately 70 percent of the natural gas supply is consumed by industries in Venezuela. In 2003, Venezuela signed a contract with neighboring Colombia, allowing the construction of a 124-mile (200 km) pipeline for natural gas distribution.

Nigeria also has an abundant supply of oil and is Africa's biggest oil exporter. Much of Nigeria's oil is found in a region called the Niger Delta; for 50 years, oil has been extracted here, potentially bringing billions of dollars into Nigeria. However, communities in the Niger Delta continue to live in poverty. This has led to incidents of oil theft where organized groups have siphoned oil from the pipelines and sold it on the black market.

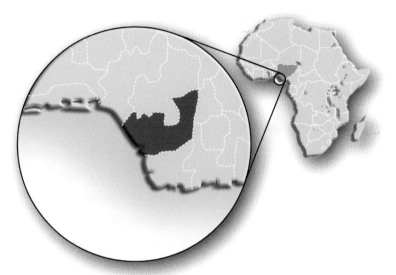

▲ Nigeria is rich in oil supplies, mainly in the delta region.

The experiences of Venezuela and Nigeria highlight the importance of local politics in deciding the cost of oil. Countries that effectively manage their products can prosper, but oil supplies do not guarantee wealth without careful planning and accountability.

The price of fuel fluctuates as events around the world influence its value. In recent years, as technology has improved and countries such as China and India have rapidly developed, energy resources are in greater demand than ever before. The demand for oil has especially increased, and because supplies are running low, oil prices have risen dramatically. Natural disasters and wars also affect the price of oil by disrupting supplies.

ENVIRONMENTAL CONCERNS

Although fossil fuels have value in financial and political terms, they impose an environmental cost. When fossil fuels are burned, their hydrocarbon molecules combust to produce steam, carbon dioxide, and carbon monoxide. Carbon dioxide is a **greenhouse gas** that contributes to global warming. Carbon monoxide is a poisonous gas that can be fatal. In addition, fossil fuels release small amounts of other gases, such as nitrogen oxides and sulfur dioxide. Nitrogen oxides produce smog and sulfur dioxide contributes to **acid rain** (see page 32).

▼ In Los Angeles, the sunny climate does not produce enough rain to clear the smog that develops from car exhaust emissions and particles in the air.

▲ Oil spills can take months, even years, to clean up.

The drilling and distribution of oil also leads to widespread destruction of the land. For example, the Caribbean coast of Venezuela is covered with oil slicks. In other parts of the country, there is **subsidence** caused by excavation programs.

FUEL CONSERVATION

Unfortunately, the decrease in fossil fuel supplies is inevitable. But there are ways to conserve fuel to make it last longer and to limit the negative effects that it has on the environment. Some governments encourage industries to conserve energy by utilizing more efficient equipment. Recycling programs are developing recycled products that are made using less energy than their "new" counterparts. Measures are being taken to reduce the amount of polluting gases that industries release into the atmosphere. These are often expensive changes for industries to make, but sometimes governments will support the industries' efforts by reducing taxes for "clean" energy users.

INVESTIGATE

▶ Photochemical smog is a type of air pollution. Use the Internet to find out how nitrogen oxides contribute to smog and the health problems that smog causes. Which cities are most affected by smog, and why?

Environmental factors

News headlines frequently warn us that the earth's temperatures are rising, glaciers are melting, and habitats are changing. But how are these stories related to the fuel that we use? Many scientists believe that recent changes in the world's climate have been caused by the rapid industrialization of our planet. And unless we take drastic action, these disturbing trends are likely to continue.

GLOBAL WARMING

Since 1900, global temperatures have risen 1.35°F (0.75°C). Moreover, since 1979, temperatures on land have increased at almost twice the rate as those on sea. In 2006, the earth experienced the warmest year on record. Unless action is taken, scientists estimate that, by 2050, temperatures may rise up to five percent each year.

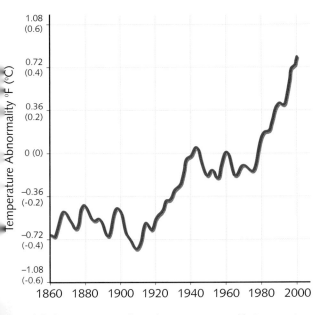

▲ Global temperatures have been rising steadily in recent years.

Scientists have been debating the urgency of global warming for years. Many scientists believe that, since the Industrial Revolution, modern human activity has drastically increased the amount of carbon dioxide in the atmosphere. Other scientists think global warming is a natural evolution in the earth's orbit around the sun. They believe that the rapid increase in atmospheric levels of carbon dioxide is not unusual and may be caused by the end of a minor ice age, which would explain the increasing temperatures and climate changes. Although the debate continues, many people want to take immediate action to reduce carbon dioxide emissions to avoid potentially serious consequences in the future.

WHY DO TEMPERATURES RISE?

It is now widely believed that increased carbon dioxide (CO_2) emissions are responsible for the rise in atmospheric temperatures. When fossil fuels burn, they release "greenhouse gases," such as CO_2, which rise into the atmosphere and form a "blanket" of gases. As a natural phenomenon, this gas blanket is very important because it helps maintain the earth's temperature at a suitable level for life to exist. However, with increased use of fossil fuels, this blanket is becoming thicker, retaining heat, and increasing temperatures on the earth.

When the sun's **radiation** passes through the atmosphere it reflects off of the earth's surface. Some of the reflected heat should escape back up into the atmosphere, but greenhouse gases are trapping the heat, causing temperatures to rise.

▼ An increase in greenhouse gases causes more of the sun's radiation to become trapped in the earth's atmosphere.

Although carbon dioxide is not the only greenhouse gas, estimates show that levels of carbon dioxide are rising 200 times faster than at any time during the last 650,000 years.

THE CONSEQUENCES OF GLOBAL WARMING

The full effects of global warming are not completely known, but scientists have made the following predictions:

▶ Effects on ecosystems—An increase in global temperatures changes sensitive **ecosystems** and forces some species out of their habitat.

▶ Glaciers—Global warming has caused glaciers to melt and become smaller. For example, the size of

the ice field on top of Mount Kilimanjaro in Tanzania has significantly decreased in recent years. Melted glaciers can also result in water shortages, causing problems for countries that rely on abundant water resources.

▲ ▼ These satellite images of Mount Kilimanjaro show a significant reduction in snow and ice at the top of the mountain between 1993 (top) and 2000 (bottom). The ice cap has lost 80 percent of its volume during the last 100 years.

▶ Ocean levels—A small rise in ocean levels can make some coastal plains uninhabitable. Scientists estimate that Vietnam, Bangladesh, and Indonesia could be seriously affected. Many port cities around the world are also under increased threat from flooding.

▲ The Thames Barrier protects London from high tides, but will it be able to stop London from flooding in the future?

▶ Ozone layer—Although chlorofluorocarbons (**CFCs**) are thought to be the main cause of the destruction of the **ozone layer**, scientists think that global warming is also weakening the ozone layer. As the earth's surface temperatures rise, the upper reaches of the atmosphere will become colder, making it more difficult for the ozone layer to repair itself. Scientists believe that by 2030, climate change may become the main cause of reduced ozone levels.

Did you know?

▶ While governments around the world are considering ways to reduce the trend of global warming, scientists are also looking at whether we can completely reverse the effects. For example, the Nobel Prize-winning chemist Paul Crutzen recently suggested that we could cool the earth by injecting sulfur into the atmosphere. Crutzen's theory is that sulfur would reflect solar radiation back into space. It is believed that this emergency climate treatment would take effect within six months and that the sulfur particles would remain in the atmosphere for up to two years. However, the consequences of this treatment—such as the risks of acid rain—are currently being investigated.

▶ Increase in biomass—An increase in carbon dioxide in the atmosphere could cause plants to increase their metabolism during **photosynthesis**. This might lead to an overabundance of dead and decaying plant matter, which would increase methane gas levels.

▶ Spread of disease—Global warming could increase the populations of disease carriers, such as rats and mosquitoes. Droughts cause a decline in predators who feed on rats and mosquitoes and changing weather patterns encourage new breeding grounds for disease carriers, who thrive in coastal or wet habitats.

▶ Financial effects—It is estimated that global warming could cost insurance companies nearly $150 billion per year in the coming decade, due to increases in flooding, forest fires, or other natural disasters.

▶ Methane gas—As sea temperatures rise at the North and South Poles methane could be released. Methane is a dangerous greenhouse gas trapped in solid, ice-like compounds found in the ocean floor. It bubbles to the surface as the water temperatures rise.

ACID RAIN

Acid rain was first reported in the UK in 1852. Despite this early report, the public was not aware of acid rain until the 1960s, when layers of glacial ice were analyzed for their gas composition. Glaciers form in layers over time—in a similar way to sedimentary rock. As glaciers form, gases from the atmosphere become trapped in the ice.

Glacier analysis has shown that levels of sulfur dioxide and nitrogen oxides in the atmosphere have increased since the Industrial Revolution. Fossil fuels contain small amounts of impurities, such as sulfur. When fuels are burned, these impurities combust in the air to form gases, such as sulfur dioxide, that rise into the atmosphere. Sulfur dioxide is a soluble gas; it will dissolve in rain clouds to form a very dilute sulfuric acid solution. This is called "acid rain." Other types of acid rain are caused by carbon dioxide, which dissolves in water to produce carbonic acid, and nitrogen oxides, which dissolve in water to produce nitric acid.

▼ When fossil fuels are burned, sulfur dioxide and nitrogen oxides are released. These gases dissolve in the atmosphere to form acid rain.

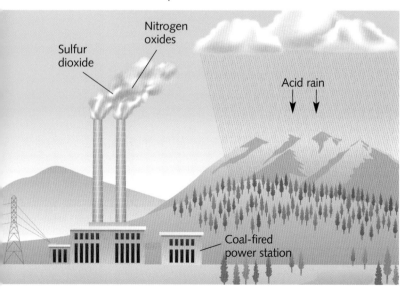

Sulfur dioxide

Nitrogen oxides

Acid rain

Coal-fired power station

THE EFFECTS OF ACID RAIN

One of the major problems with acid rain is that it is not always a localized problem; prevailing winds can easily carry it to other areas. Acid rain corrodes buildings and structures, and is damaging to ecosystems:

▶ Lakes—Scientists have shown that there is a strong link between acidic water and declining populations of fish. Acidic water prevents key **enzymes** from working in fish larvae, causing their deaths. Acid rain also releases toxic metals—such as aluminum—into lakes, causing some fish to produce excess mucus that interferes with their gills' functioning. Simple plankton will also not grow in acidic water, creating a major disruption in the food chain.

▲ These freshwater plankton form the basis of a river food chain, but acid rain is causing a decline in their numbers.

▲ Acid rain damages trees because it reacts with nutrients in the soil that the trees need to survive.

▶ Trees—Acid rain is damaging to trees; the wax on the leaves breaks down, root growth slows, and toxic metals are ingested by the trees.

▶ Soil—Acid rain can leach minerals out of the soil, making it unsuitable for plants to grow.

▶ Buildings and statues—Stonework, such as that made from limestone, contains calcium that reacts with sulfuric acid. This type of corrosion is often seen on gravestones and churchyard statues.

▶ Microorganisms—Some tropical microorganisms readily consume acids, but others cannot survive in acidic conditions. This affects the natural balance in ecosystems.

▶ Metals—Acid rain causes rust to form on metals containing iron because the acid accelerates the **oxidation** process.

We reduce acid rain by limiting levels of polluting gases in the atmosphere. Two simple measures are using low-sulfur gasoline or diesel in cars and installing catalytic converters to reduce levels of nitrogen dioxide emitted from the exhaust. Long-term solutions include burning fewer fossil fuels and using alternate sources of energy.

MONITORING AIR QUALITY

Monitoring air quality has become an important science. Some governments set targets for improving air quality and pass legislation, such as the Clean Air Act in the U.S. Countries have monitoring sites that keep track of nationwide pollution levels. Automatic monitoring networks record pollution on a regular basis to detect any changing patterns. Scientists also look at specific pollutants affecting urban and rural areas. Two main methods are used to monitor air quality:

▶ Passive sampling—Passive sampling is an inexpensive air monitoring method, often used to detect nitrogen dioxide and benzene. Sampling tubes are open to the atmosphere. The open end of the tube faces toward the ground to prevent any rain or dust from entering the tube. They are called "passive" because air samples flow through the sampling tube by **diffusion**. Samples of the air are collected and analyzed in a laboratory.

▶ Active sampling—In active sampling, a particular volume of air is pumped through a collector over a set period of time, and the samples are collected daily. This type of sampling is commonly used for ozone, nitrogen oxides, sulfur dioxide, and carbon monoxide. The air samples are analyzed using spectroscopy to produce an accurate picture of the quantity and type of pollution that they contain.

INDICATOR SPECIES

Particular pollutants affect certain living organisms. For example, lichens are sensitive to sulfur dioxide. Since the Industrial Revolution, lichen species have dramatically decreased. Lichens absorb sulfur dioxide, which then accumulates inside the plants and causes irreversible damage.

Lichens are **bioindicators** because they indicate the amount of sulfur dioxide present in air. Some lichens are more tolerant of sulfur dioxide than others, so observing which lichen species are present in an area can help evaluate air quality levels. Bioindicators are used to monitor water pollution, too. For example, the presence of a lot of salmon or trout in a river indicates clean water.

◀ These sensors are used to measure air pollution levels. They are placed by roads or industrial plants to measure the pollution caused by vehicles or factory emissions.

Fuel of the future

Modern lifestyles demand more and more energy. Yet, fossil fuels will not last forever. With the ongoing decline in fossil fuels, scientists continue to search for new sources of energy that are inexpensive and safe for the environment. Some energy alternatives may be nuclear energy, wind or solar energy, and hydrogen gas.

HYDROGEN – THE FUEL OF THE FUTURE?

Hydrogen is considered a viable alternative to fossil fuels. Hydrogen is present in many substances, but the most common source of hydrogen is water (H_2O). The oceans could provide an endless supply of hydrogen fuel. Hydrogen is also a "clean" source of energy. When hydrogen burns, it does not pollute the atmosphere because the only combustion product is water. Hydrogen is very light, and it releases a great deal of energy. For this reason, it is ideal for use in spacecraft because a relatively small amount of fuel can supply enough power for a long journey.

▲ Hydrogen gas could be an economical way to keep this space shuttle in orbit for long periods of time.

Hydrogen can also power cars. Instead of a traditional combustion engine that releases pollutants such as carbon dioxide, hydrogen cars use a hydrogen **fuel cell**. While batteries use a limited amount of stored energy, fuel cells use external substances, such as hydrogen and oxygen, and they continue to work as long as a fuel source is available. Hydrogen is stored in the vehicle and is mixed with oxygen from the air to generate heat and electricity in a chemical reaction. Water is also produced during this process. The electricity runs the engine to power the wheels. Fuel cells are about 50 percent more efficient than the average internal combustion engine. Hydrogen also burns more safely than gasoline.

THE DISADVANTAGES OF HYDROGEN

▶ Although hydrogen is plentiful in the form of water, it has to be separated from water using a process called **electrolysis**. This is very expensive.

▶ Hydrogen is a clean fuel but the energy needed for electrolysis comes from burning fossil fuels, which are polluting.

▶ Currently, fuel cells are very expensive, so hydrogen cars are not easily affordable.

▶ Unless hydrogen gas is compressed and liquefied, large tanks are required to store and transport it.

▶ Energy is needed to compress hydrogen gas, and the compressed gas is not as efficient. Compression also carries the risk of explosion. To overcome this risk, special reinforced tanks are constructed, further increasing the price of hydrogen.

▲ These hydrogen gas tanks are used to store compressed hydrogen gas safely, but the tanks are expensive.

CURRENT PROGRAMS

Some countries are taking hydrogen fuel very seriously. Sweden is planning to be oil-free within the next 20 years and will rely solely on alternate energy sources, such as hydrogen. Iceland is committed to becoming the world's first hydrogen-fueled economy by 2050. Iceland currently imports all of its hydrocarbon energy sources. However, Iceland also has a large **geothermal** resource that makes the cost of electricity in Iceland cheaper than the price of imported hydrocarbons. Therefore, surplus electricity in Iceland is converted into hydrocarbon replacements, such as hydrogen. Since 2002, Iceland has produced around 2,205 tons (2,000 t) of hydrogen every year.

Another alternative fuel pilot project is taking place on a Norwegian island. Wind power is generating hydrogen, which is then stored. When there is little wind available, the hydrogen power is used as an alternate energy source.

In December 2005, the UK introduced fuel cell buses in central London. These buses create less pollution than conventional buses. Other fuel cell buses are now being used in Europe and the U.S. If the drawbacks of hydrogen can be resolved, it could be a viable fuel for the future.

▲ This bus in Iceland is powered by a fuel cell that runs on hydrogen gas.

DID YOU KNOW?

▶ In 2005, 61 million tons (55 million t) of hydrogen were produced globally. This is the equivalent of around 209 million tons (190 million t) of oil. Hydrogen production is expected to rise about 10 percent every year.

▶ An American company has successfully completed test flights for an aircraft operating completely on liquid hydrogen. The hydrogen is stored onboard and oxygen is collected during the flight. Together, these gases react in fuel cells to generate the power needed to propel the aircraft. The company claims that one tank of fuel will keep the aircraft airborne for 24 hours.

TEST YOURSELF

▶ We burn fossil fuels to create the energy needed to separate hydrogen from water. What other sources of energy could be used that are safer for the environment?

GASOHOL AND HYBRID CARS

Some countries make better use of their gasoline by mixing it with 10 percent ethanol to form a mixture called gasohol. This mixture is sometimes called E10 and can be used in car engines without any extra adaptation. Denmark, for example, uses the fuel nationwide and Brazil now produces over 4.2 billion gallons (16 billion l) of ethanol—using half its sugar harvest to fuel cars.

MAKING GASOHOL

Until 1975, Brazil relied heavily on imported oil to meet its growing energy needs. However, with the increasing price of oil, the Brazilian government decided to invest in gasohol production.

The glucose in sugar cane is converted into ethanol through the process of fermentation. This process is cheaper than obtaining ethanol from the fractional distillation of alcohol solutions. Brazilian farmers are awarded generous subsidies for growing sugar cane.

The equation for this reaction is as follows:

Glucose $\longrightarrow$ Ethanol + Carbon dioxide

$$C_6H_{12}O_{6(s)} \longrightarrow 2C_2H_5OH_{(l)} + 2CO_{2(g)}$$

Brazil has a hot, tropical climate and sugar cane grows easily there. However, ethanol production is not viable in all countries because it depends on favorable weather conditions.

HYBRID CARS

A hybrid vehicle is one that has its own onboard rechargeable energy storage system. For example, mopeds combine the power of gasoline with the pedal power of the rider. Trains are commonly diesel-electric hybrids. In Seattle, overhead electric wires power diesel-electric buses. Some cars are gasoline-electric hybrids.

All cars should be able to drive over 248 miles (400 km) before refueling, and they should be easy to refuel. Also, they should be able to keep up with other traffic on the road. Gasoline and diesel cars meet these requirements, but they also produce a lot of pollution. A hybrid car significantly reduces the amount of greenhouse gas emissions, while also meeting these performance standards.

HOW DO THEY WORK?

A hybrid car works in one of two ways.
(1) It uses either stored gasoline or stored electricity in a battery to start the motor. Once the motor is running, both the gasoline and the electricity are used to power the vehicle.
(2) Gasoline turns a generator but the car is powered by electricity. The generator produces electricity for storage in the car's batteries.

DID YOU KNOW?

▶ Ethanol is also produced from the fermentation of corn. However, some people think this is a waste of food. The amount of corn needed to fill a 16-gallon (60 l) fuel tank with ethanol would feed one person for six months.

▶ About 55 million tons (50 million t) of U.S. corn goes into ethanol production every year. This is nearly one-sixth of the country's grain harvest, but will supply only 3 percent of its demand for vehicle fuel.

▲ Wind farms tend to be located in remote, flat, or high-elevation areas where winds are strong and urban areas are least affected.

THE POWER OF NATURE

Natural energy sources, such as wind and tidal energy, have been developed over recent years as a potential source of clean energy. At present, these energy sources do not produce large amounts of electricity, and it is difficult to persuade governments to use them. This may change as fossil fuel supplies dwindle and the search for clean energy sources becomes more important than ever.

WIND POWER

In 2005, wind power contributed approximately one percent of the world's energy supply. Wind power is generated through large turbines that convert wind-powered movement into electricity through a generator. Since the 1890s, wind energy has provided power. For example, windmills have been used to crush grain or pump water.

▲ Windmills have traditionally been used to capture energy. They use the power of the wind to turn machinery.

ADVANTAGES AND DISADVANTAGES

Wind energy is a good alternate energy source because it does not rely on fossil fuels or produce polluting gases. This source of energy is also unlikely to run out and the electricity that it generates can be stored for later use. However, a large number of wind turbines are needed to produce a significant amount of electricity. Many people think that groups of turbines (or "wind farms") are ugly and spoil the landscape. For this reason, many wind turbines are located on the oceans, away from urban activity. The turbines also pose a danger to migrating birds that accidentally fly into them. Wind turbines are built in areas where the wind speed is greater than 12 miles (20 km) per hour. These areas tend to be at high altitudes, on flat surfaces, or out at sea.

Germany, Spain, India, Denmark, and the U.S. currently have the largest investments in wind power. Denmark also has a large market in wind turbine exports.

WATER

Water is a natural resource that can be transformed into electrical power. Water power currently comprises around one-sixth of the world's electricity. In a **hydroelectric** power station, river water is collected by a dam and flows through turbines to generate electricity. Power stations also use ocean water to generate electricity, capturing the power of the waves or the tides that move across the ocean.

ADVANTAGES AND DISADVANTAGES

Water is another renewable source of energy that can generate significant amounts of power. For example, if a proposed dam on the Severn estuary in the UK is built, it is estimated that 19.8 million tons (18 million t) of coal could be saved for every year the dam is in operation.

However, hydroelectric power also has drawbacks. Dams stop fish and other animals from moving up and down rivers. Changes in the flow of water also cause salt levels and the amount of sunlight that penetrates the water to change. These factors have

TEST YOURSELF

▶ Prepare a table listing the advantages and disadvantages of each of the alternative energy sources described on pages 35–45.

a significant effect on the food chain. Dams also cause flooding. When plants become submerged by floodwater they decompose quickly, releasing methane gas—a greenhouse gas thought to contribute to global warming.

▼ Large ocean turbines use the energy of moving water to generate electricity.

GEOTHERMAL ENERGY

Geothermal energy—the heat from the earth's crust—can be used to generate electricity. In some parts of the world, there are hot rocks beneath the earth's surface. Water pipes are passed through the hot rocks or cold water is pumped into the ground to absorb the heat, which creates hot water for homes.

In other countries, such as Iceland, thermal pools are utilized. Wells are drilled and the upward flow of hot water or steam is used to generate electricity. It is estimated that Iceland can produce significant amounts of geothermal energy for another 100 years.

Changing levels of heat in the world's oceans can also be used to generate power. The oceans absorb energy from the sun and this makes surface waters warmer than deeper waters. A new technology called Ocean Thermal Energy Conversion (OTEC) uses these differences in temperatures to generate electricity.

ADVANTAGES AND DISADVANTAGES

Geothermal power is produced cost-effectively in areas such as Africa. For example, in Kenya, two large geothermal plants have been built, with plans for a third. Together, these facilities provide an estimated 25 percent of Kenya's energy demands and they reduce the country's reliance on imported oil.

However, using geothermal energy can cause minor movements in the earth's crust and could increase the risk of earthquakes. This is particularly the case if cold water is injected into the ground. Also, the cooling effect of the water makes the geothermal energy a less efficient renewable resource.

SOLAR POWER

The amount of energy reaching the earth from the sun each day is around 10,000 times the world's current daily energy demand. Some of this energy can be captured to make electricity. Solar cells absorb the sun's radiation and release **electrons**, creating an electric current. Solar energy also heats water circulating in pipes. The pipes are painted a nonreflective black, to absorb as much radiation as possible. Today, the amount of solar energy that can be collected is limited. This may change in the coming years as technology develops. Some houses are built with solar panels on the roof to supplement traditional electrical energy. In the future, even cars may run on solar power.

▲ Solar panels produce extra electricity for a home.

TIME TRAVEL: INTO THE FUTURE

▶ Solar energy is currently used in space to power spacecraft and satellites. The energy is captured using solar panels similar to those described on this page. Scientists think that in the future, solar satellites might be able to gather solar energy and send it back to the earth using microwave beams. If this solar energy is converted into electricity, it could be an endless supply of clean power.

NUCLEAR POWER

In 1896, nuclear energy was accidentally discovered by the French scientist Antoine-Henri Becquerel. Becquerel found some photographic plates that had been stored near uranium and noticed they were changed in ways similar to that of light exposure. This discovery paved the way for many years of research, leading to today's use of nuclear energy as a source of electricity.

▲ A.H. Becquerel

▲ Nuclear power stations currently generate about 17 percent of the world's electricity.

WHAT IS NUCLEAR POWER?

The neutrons and protons in the nucleus of an atom are held together by very strong forces. When a heavy nucleus is split, these forces are released as energy. This is called **nuclear fission** and is the type of nuclear energy produced in most power stations. Energy is also produced when two lighter nuclei are joined. We call this **nuclear fusion**.

Nuclear energy is produced by a fuel called uranium. Uranium is found in rocks in the ground but has to be refined before it can be used as nuclear fuel. Nuclear energy is generated in a nuclear reactor, a large tank or building inside a nuclear power station. Here, uranium atoms are split or fused to release energy. If the atoms split, particles are released. These particles strike other uranium atoms, causing them to split, too. The reactions in power stations are carried out in controlled conditions at a steady rate.

The energy released heats water to make steam that spins a turbine. The spinning turbine powers a generator to produce electricity. Some countries, such as France, depend on nuclear energy for most of their electricity. Other governments find it difficult to balance the advantages and disadvantages of nuclear power. However, with an urgent need to find alternatives to fossil fuels, nuclear power may become more popular.

ADVANTAGES

▶ Although nuclear reactors are very expensive to build, only a small amount of fuel is needed to produce nuclear energy—2.2 pounds (1 kg) of uranium produces as much energy as 3,307 tons (3,000 t) of coal! Once a reactor is established, nuclear power can be considered a relatively inexpensive source of electricity.

▶ Nuclear energy is considered a clean source of energy because it does not produce polluting gases.

▶ Nuclear power stations help countries maintain energy independence rather than rely on imports from other countries.

▶ Nuclear energy does not rely on weather patterns, which are essential for wind or solar power.

DISADVANTAGES

▶ Many people worry about the safety of nuclear energy, particularly after high-profile disasters such as the accident at Chernobyl in Ukraine. Safety standards have greatly improved over the last 30 years, but there is still concern about the hazards of nuclear power.

▼ In 1986, human error caused a meltdown in the Chernobyl nuclear reactor in Ukraine; this was the world's worst nuclear disaster.

▶ Mining for uranium scars the natural landscape. Large quantities of rock have to be mined in order to find small deposits of uranium. This destroys natural habitats.

▶ Fossil fuels are used in part of nuclear production—for mining, transportation, and waste disposal.

▶ Nuclear waste remains radioactive, and dangerous, for thousands of years. Managing this waste is problematic and very expensive. Nuclear waste must be stored in special containers to avoid contact with water. If nuclear waste contacted the water, the waste could rust. Like the nuclear waste, the rust would be radioactive and could contaminate the water supply.

▶ Power stations are targets for terrorist attacks. The materials used in nuclear fuel are highly radioactive and they make people very ill. Security at nuclear power stations must be very strict. Nuclear technology can be easily adapted to produce nuclear weapons that cause massive devastation.

NUCLEAR WASTE

Nuclear reactors produce materials that cannot be used again. Unfortunately, these materials remain radioactive for thousands of years. Nuclear fuels are first cooled in special ponds in the nuclear power station, which can take up to 50 years! Once they are cooled, the fuels are dissolved in acid so that they can be disposed of safely. The waste is then turned into powder and stored in strong metal containers.

A more permanent solution to the nuclear waste problem is to bury the waste deep underground. The Canadian government is considering a plan

▲ These fuel rods are being cooled in a special pond at a nuclear power station.

to dig a vault, within stable geological formations, 1,640 to 3,281 feet (500–1,000 m) underground. Nuclear waste would be stored in these vaults, in corrosion-resistant containers. In the U.S., there are also plans to bury nuclear waste in the Nevada Desert. However, local residents are worried about having radioactive materials in the area.

▶ Some nuclear waste is turned into a dry powder and stored in strong metal containers. Nuclear waste storage sites are not popular with area residents.

One of the more exciting areas of research into renewable fuels is the use of biomass—energy from the sun that is incorporated into animals and plants through the food chain. Biomass fuels (or "biofuels") can be burned to release energy. Although the technology is still being developed, biofuels have the potential to become a widespread source of renewable and clean energy.

SOURCES OF BIOFUELS

Plant resources, such as wood, straw, and charcoal, are an abundant source of biofuels. Some crops are specifically grown for the production of biofuels. These include corn, soybeans, and rapeseed.

▲ These soybean pods contain usable energy.

▲ These wood chips are used for biofuel production.

Although these fuels release carbon dioxide when they are burned, they also absorb carbon dioxide as they grow. This balances the amount of carbon dioxide in the atmosphere.

Vegetable and animal fats are also a source of biofuel. Vegetable oils come from seeds, nuts, and fruits, such as sunflower seeds, peanuts, and olives, and many animals store fat under their skin. Biofuels can also be made from waste material, such as animal feces, forestry waste, or household trash, providing a useful answer to some of the world's waste management problems.

Ocean plants are also used as biofuels. Seaweed, such as *Sargassum* and *Zostera,* can grow up to 24 inches (60 cm) per day. Scientists think that huge seaweed farms could absorb vast quantities of carbon dioxide during photosynthesis and then be harvested as a source of biofuel.

▼ Rapeseed is another common source of biofuel.

▼ *Sargassum* seaweed grows very quickly.

USES FOR BIOFUELS

Biofuel sources currently generate approximately 15 percent of the world's energy. Biofuels are most commonly used for domestic cooking and heating. For example, some homeowners in the U.S. burn corn in special stoves to reduce their home heating bills. Biofuels, such as biogas, can generate electricity. Biogas is made from animal and human waste and rotting plant matter. The gas can even be collected from rotting waste material in compost heaps or landfill sites. Biogas is mostly methane. It can be used for heating and lighting, but it mainly generates electricity.

THE ADVANTAGES OF BIOFUELS

▶ Using biofuels saves nonrenewable energy resources such as coal, oil, and gas.

▶ Biofuels are made from a variety of natural resources. Biodiesel—fuel used in vehicles—is made from palm, cottonseed, sunflower, and peanut oil. Biodiesel can also be made from recycled cooking grease!

▶ Biofuels emit low levels of greenhouse gases when they are burned.

▶ When biofuels are used as car fuel they are very efficient, improving mileage by up to three percent. They also produce less exhaust emissions. Biodiesel can be used in any diesel engine with very little modification.

▶ Biofuels can be stored for long periods of time without loss of energy.

▶ Crops can be grown continuously, which means biofuels are renewable. This also helps the agricultural community. Crops absorb carbon dioxide (CO_2) when they grow, balancing the amount of CO_2 released when they are burned.

▶ Biofuels could reduce dependency on foreign oil imports.

▶ Biofuels are biodegradable—if they are spilled or buried in the ground, they easily decompose.

▲ Biofuels are safer for the environment than traditional fossil fuels.

THE DISADVANTAGES OF BIOFUELS

▶ Biofuels are unreliable when used at both high and low temperatures. They decompose when they are hot, and they may solidify when cold. This would be a problem for vehicles that depend on biofuel.

▶ Biodiesel is a type of biofuel made from crops such as corn, sunflowers, or soybeans. As biodiesel passes through a car engine, it deposits particles that clog filters. Biodiesel can also corrode rubber components.

▶ Biofuels release methane gas. This is a greenhouse gas that contributes to global warming.

▶ Biofuels are expensive to produce. Soybean oil and rapeseed oil are currently the only inexpensive source of biofuel.

MODIFYING BIOFUELS

Despite their advantages, biofuels are not used as a major source of energy in many countries because the convenience of fossil fuels, such as oil and gas, makes them a more appealing short-term option. Scientists are trying to modify biofuels to make them more convenient. Researchers at the U.S. department of Agriculture have successfully modified soybean oil to make it more effective at varying temperatures. In the coming years, other modifications to biofuels may make them indispensable to future generations.

Glossary

ACID RAIN – Rain that contains high levels of nitric or sulfuric acid. Acid rain forms when gases from industrial fuels combine with moisture in the atmosphere.

BIODEGRADABLE – The decomposition of material through the action of organisms.

BIOINDICATORS – Biological species that cannot tolerate certain levels of pollution.

BIOMASS – Dead organisms used for fuel.

CFCS – Chlorofluorocarbons. CFCs are chemical compounds widely used in industry. When CFCs enter the atmosphere, they release chlorine which causes damage to the earth's ozone layer.

COMBUSTION REACTION – A burning reaction.

COMPOUND – A substance consisting of two (or more) elements chemically bonded.

CONDENSE – To change from a gas to a liquid. Condensation occurs when gases are cooled.

CRUDE OIL – Unrefined oil.

DIFFUSION – The movement of particles from areas of high concentration to areas of low concentration.

ECOSYSTEM – A collection of living things and the environment in which they live.

ELECTROLYSIS – Using electricity to decompose chemical compounds.

ELECTRON – The negatively charged part of an atom.

ENZYMES – Proteins in living organisms that accelerate chemical reactions.

FERMENTATION – A reaction in which sugar is converted into alcohol.

FOOD CHAIN – The way in which a series of organisms depend on each other for sources of food.

FOSSIL FUELS – Fuels that derive from the fossilized remains of prehistoric plants and animals. Coal, oil, and gas are fossil fuels.

ANSWERS

Page 17: Investigate
You should find that paraffin produces more energy than ethanol.

Page 19: Test yourself
(1) The lighter fractions separated sooner than the darker fractions, so they contain fewer carbon atoms.

(2) Use the table on page 19 to check your answer.

Page 23: Test yourself
The refinery is best placed on the east side of the port. This location is close to transportation routes and would have an abundance of workers from the city nearby. Oil that is extracted at sea could be transported to the refinery easily. If the refinery was placed here, the prevailing winds would also blow the refinery fumes out to sea.

Page 26: Test yourself
The cost of plastic is a result of the cost of oil that it is derived from. Oil prices have risen due to war, dwindling supplies, and increased demand.

Page 28: Investigate
Sunlight and emissions such as nitrogen oxide react producing a fine film known as smog. This hangs low over areas where the chemicals are produced. The smog can cause respiratory problems in some people.

Cities, such as London and Los Angeles, where there are a lot of traffic fumes, are most affected. Cities such as Los Angeles also have a sunny climate and small amounts of rain. Rain helps clear smog from the air.

Page 33: Test yourself
Prevailing winds carry clouds containing acid rain from countries west of Scandinavia, such as the UK.

Page 37: Test yourself
Other sources of energy could be developed, such as nuclear energy, solar energy, wind energy, and water energy.

Page 39: Test yourself
Answers can be found in the text but may include some of the following factors:

Advantages: plentiful; clean; light; renewable; cost-effective; reduced reliance on fossil fuels; made from waste material; reduced risk of greenhouse gases, global warming, and damage to the ozone layer.

FUEL CELL – A device, like a battery, that generates electricity through a chemical reaction. Fuel cells use external substances, such as hydrogen and oxygen.

GEOTHERMAL – The internal heat of the earth.

GLOBAL WARMING – The warming of the earth's climate, thought to be caused by gases in the atmosphere trapping heat from the sun.

GREENHOUSE GAS – A gas that contributes to global warming, such as carbon dioxide or methane.

HYDROCARBONS – Compounds that contain only hydrogen and carbon atoms.

HYDROELECTRICITY – Electricity generated by the energy of running water. Hydroelectric power stations use dams to capture and store large quantities of water.

METHANE – A gas made from carbon and hydrogen that can be used as a fuel.

NONBIODEGRADABLE – A substance that takes many hundreds of years to break down.

Disadvantages: expensive; may still rely on burning polluting fossil fuels for extraction; not easily stored or transported; unreliable; can be dangerous; limited availability; unable to produce significant amounts of energy; damages the natural landscape; risk of damage to local wildlife or the balance of ecosystems; may depend on weather patterns (e.g. wind, solar).

NONRENEWABLE – A substance that is not easily replaced.

NUCLEAR FISSION – The process of splitting an atom's nucleus in two to release energy.

NUCLEAR FUSION – The process of joining two atoms' nuclei to release energy.

OXIDATION – A chemical reaction in which oxygen is gained.

OZONE LAYER – A part of the atmosphere, at an altitude of about 9.3 to 18.6 miles (15–30 km), containing ozone. Ozone is a gas that absorbs ultraviolet radiation from the sun.

PHOTOSYNTHESIS – The process in green plants in which carbon dioxide is converted into oxygen.

POLYMERIZATION – A process for making plastics.

RADIATION – The transmission of energy through space. Energy from the sun that travels to the earth is an example of radiation.

RECYCLING – The process of reusing materials.

REFINE – The process of purifying a substance.

SPECTROSCOPY – The study of light energy and radiation in matter.

SUBSIDENCE – When part of the land sinks due to large-scale earth removal or underground excavations.

TOXIC – Capable of causing injury or death by poison.

Useful Web sites:
www.eia.doe.gov/kids/
www.chem4kids.com
www.sciencenewsforkids.org
www.howstuffworks.com
www.pbs.org/wnet/extremeoil/index.html

Index